JUNIOR

HABITUDE WARRIORS

Guide to Building Confidence, Leadership, & Personal Development

By ERIK SWANSON

&

His Contributing Expert Co-Authors

JUNIOR HABITUDE WARRIORS
by ERIK SWANSON

& The Junior Habitude Warrior Expert Contributing Co-Authors:

Larayne Glidewell, Joshua Evans, Jason Freeman, Jenya Carter, Melisa Hall, Sharon Lechter, Steve Beckles-Ebusua, Scott Sorrell, Dali Melo, Ryan Lowe, Stacey Ellen, Justin Renner, Eric Lassard, Chris Warner, & Logan Langemeier.

This publication was printed in the United States of America!

Published by Habitude Warrior, International
Erik Swanson
www.JuniorHabitudeWarrior.com

In association with:
Elite Online Publishing
Sandy, UT 84070
www.EliteOnlinePublishing.com

ISBN-13: 978-1979372039
ISBN-10: 1979372039

Meet Our Habitude Warrior Coach

Erik Swanson has delivered over 6000 motivational presentations at conferences and meetings worldwide. As an award winning International Keynote Speaker, Best-Selling Author & Attitude Coach, Erik Swanson is in great demand! Speaking on average to more than one million people per year, he is both versatile in his approach and effective in a wide array of training topics.

Respectively nicknamed "*MR. AWESOME*" by many who know him well, Erik invites some of the most talented and most famous speakers of the world to join him on his coveted stages, such as Brian Tracy, Nasa's Performance Coach Dr. Denis Waitley,

Motivational Legend Les Brown… From the book & movie 'The Secret,' Bob Proctor, Jack Canfield, John Assaraf, & The Millionaire Maker Loral Langemeier, Co-Author of 'Rich Dad Poor Dad' Sharon Lechter. Mr. Swanson has created and developed the super popular *Habitude Warrior Conference* which boasts a 2-year waiting list and includes over 33 top leaders around the world in a 'Ted Talk' style event, which has quickly climbed to one of the top 10 events not to miss in the United States!

Tell us more about "Junior Habitude Warrior" Conferences:

"If you are looking for a place for your children to learn the secrets of success to build upon their future, then look no further. Junior Habitude Warriors is the place to send them!"

- Claudia Soul - The Clarity Doctor

"Sign your children up for this program, and you will thank me!"

- Michael Contello - Father

"As a Mom, my absolute #1 priority are my children. I'm so glad there are associations like the Junior Habitude Warriors! They teach our children the importance of courage, confidence, and leadership."

- Roxie Albritton Lansford - Mother

"As a teacher and mentor, I know the value and importance for our youth to learn and build the best habits of success at an early age. The Junior Habitude Warriors program does exactly that! Thank you!"

- Larayne Glidewell - Mentor

"One of the best decisions I had made was to bring my teen to learn at the Junior Habitude Warrior Conference."

- Johnny Morney Jr. - Father .

Junior Habitude Warrior Conferences

Created and developed by Erik "Mr. Awesome" Swanson and his team of experts, the Junior Habitude Warrior Conference is a 1-day success camp geared towards kids ages 8 to 18 where we have our experts teach and coach throughout the day in these 3 categories: Confidence, Leadership & Personal Development. These are areas that schools, unfortunately, neglect to teach our kids these days. To nominate a child to be considered, please apply at:

www.JuniorHabitudeWarrior.com

"Your thoughts determine your attitude. Your attitude determines your habits. Your *'HABITUDES'* determine your future!"

-Erik "Mr. Awesome" Swanson

Introduction: Hey Parents!

Welcome to a collaboration of experts from around the world! I have personally sought out the brightest, smartest, and the most awesomest coaches from around the globe to teach, so join me in teaching you, and your children, the principles in becoming a *Junior Habitude Warrior*. What does it mean to have that designation? Well, it means that you have mastered the art of building amazing habits of success while maintaining an awesome, daily positive attitude as well. Our experts assist me in teaching the fundamentals of success in these three categories: Confidence, Leadership and Personal Development. It's time to help our children learn these vital principles that are sometimes neglected in schools these days.

We view this book as more of a blueprint or workbook to dive into each lesson together with your children to get the most out of it. There are fun assignments and strategies you will want to encounter together as you grow within a chapter and lesson. We also really look forward to meeting your children at one of our upcoming Junior Habitude Warrior events. Look for them at: www.JuniorHabitudeWarrior.com

~ Erik Swanson

Introduction:
Hey Cool Kids!

I'm super glad you're picking this book up and reading it right now. It's going to be a ton of fun. Now, here's the deal... this book is all about **you**. It's about building awesome skills of success to make you even more awesome than you already are!

Take as many notes as you can and complete each of the assignments and exercises. Trust me, they are fun. You can work with your parents within each of the exercises to get them involved as well. In fact, we are going to talk to them about setting up some cool awards and rewards for you if you actually involve your parents with this book. So, start to think of some cool goals and rewards you would like to accomplish and have.

By learning and applying these secrets of success at your early age, life is going to be so much easier for you to succeed once you master these principles laid out in this book. In fact, we would love to see you at one of our big events in the future called the Junior

Habitude Warrior events. See you there! Okay, let's rock-n-roll now! ~ Erik Swanson

TABLE OF CONTENTS

1

THREE SKILLS WE MUST HAVE

Welcome! I'm so excited you are here. My name is Erik, and I'll be guiding you through the journey of this book. You'll find this book is very similar to having a conversation. That's the easiest way to learn, and quite frankly, it's the easiest way I know how to teach. The truth is, when I younger I found it very difficult to focus in school and I never wanted to read any books. Boy, was that a mistake. A big mistake. I allowed others to pass me by and do much better than me in school. I didn't learn the lesson until later on in life that I should have paid more attention to those trying to teach me the principles of success. One of the best things you can do as a child or a teen, rather than going out and playing all the time, is to sit down and learn from books that will teach you solid principles of success to live an amazing life!

The more success books you read today will virtually guarantee that you will have a more fulfilling and abundant life later, provided that you take action on the principles that you learn in those books.

There's a great saying:

The more you learn, the more you earn!

I love that saying. In fact, we have a proposition to the parents reading this book right now, (Kids, hang tight. Let me chat with your parents for a second). Parents: So, here's a GREAT idea! Rather than just rewarding your kids for doing chores around the house, why not reward them for completing a success book. No kid is going to get rich off of washing the dishes or taking the trash out each night. But, by reading a success book such as this one or many others we can recommend for them to read, now we're talking… and they will have an amazing edge to succeed in life, business, entrepreneurship, and personal growth. Here's an idea that we suggest to a lot of our coaching client parents. For every success book, your child reads, completes and does a book report for you, you reward them with a $20 bill! At first, it may take them a few weeks to complete one book. Then, once they get the hang of it and develop that *'Junior Habitude Warrior'* habit, they will be able to complete a book every-other-week. It's well worth the money for you to invest in your child and such an amazing education for your child! Give this technique a shot and let us know how it turns out. We are sure you and your child will be very happy!

Okay, cool kids, I'm back! So, let's get started.

The 3 Skills We Must Have

We all must have 3 major skills to be successful in life these days. Here are the 3 skills:

Confidence, Leadership, and Personal Development.

These 3 skills will assist you in every area of your life. Let's develop our habits in all 3 of them by the end of this book and practice each of them each day of the rest of our lives. To truly master a skill is to continue to learn and grow within that skill each and every day, constantly improving. There is a saying: *Success leaves clues!* This is so true. And that is why we have invited our expert friends who are really cool as well to help us in each of these 3 subjects throughout this book. Take notes. Ask questions. Do the assignments and exercises. Talk to your parents about each chapter so that you get them involved as much as you can. (Also, ask them about the Book Report Reward!)

2

CONFIDENCE

The main definition of the word *Confidence* is to believe in yourself. To be sure of yourself in a good way. When you are confident, you walk a little differently. You feel a little different. You start to smile a lot more throughout the day. People will start to notice that you have more of a bounce in your step when you walk. You start to hold your head up a little higher, with a smile on your face. You don't allow other's to get your mood down. You don't allow other's opinions of you affect you at all. You tend to see life in a more positive light.

Keep in mind, being confident is a positive thing. It's very different than being *conceited*. The sign of a true champion is one who can hold their head up high in confidence, in a classy way... always striving to help others feel great about themselves as well. It is a very attractive quality to have confidence. Let's try this exercise for the rest of this week. I want you to choose to smile any chance you get. That's right. Try it now. Just throw a smile to anyone and everyone you see for the week.

3

CONFIDENCE IS LISTENING TO YOUR OWN INTUITION

By Larayne Glidewell

In our lives there are so many people around us (parents, teachers, bosses, elders, peers) telling us what to do, where to go, and how to do things as we grow up. We begin to rely on the outside world to make decisions for us and to check with these people to make sure we're on the right path. We start to see this often show up in little kids ages 6 months to 2 years old. From the early start of looking back to our parents for approval for everything, we are taught to constantly look to others in our lives for that same approval to see if we are doing something right or wrong. After experiencing this in school and in life, it can become confusing to figure out how to look internally (your own intuition) to make your own choices and to be confident with those decisions that we ultimately make. From something as simple as picking out the right clothes to wear for school, the right college education, and even the right career path to take. Sometimes, on days I'm not feeling confident in my choices, I will occasionally text a picture of an outfit to a friend of mine before going to an important meeting just to make sure it looks good. We all have our days that we lack some of that confidence. In these chapters of this book, you have experts who will help guide you to learn the secrets to building confidence.

Let me share some ideas. How do you build the confidence in your own choices without looking to someone else's opinions or knowledge? How do you build that self-belief within to know what steps to take on your own? To start, I invite you to look within yourself. Believe that you are great, special, capable, and good enough! Taking steps each day in these areas creates a foundation to build your own steps in being confident in what you are doing in your life. I like to start each morning reminding myself about my value and true worth with what is called 'mirror work.' Looking at my own eyes in the mirror and saying affirmations as I get dressed in the morning. This starts my day off in such a positive way and reminds me of my capabilities in believing in myself. What are affirmations? Affirmations are little sayings that you tell yourself to build up your confidence and self-esteem.

Here are some affirmations…

I love myself!

I make good choices.

My best is good enough.

I am loved, and I am a lovable person.

God always takes care of everything I need.

I am surrounded by loving people

Everything works out for my best self

I am smart

I am safe

I am great

I am beautiful

I am worthy of joy

I am joyful

I am filled with happiness

I am perfect the way I am

Getting connected with yourself can look different within each of us. Each of us is born with our own gifts and talents. If you aren't certain what your gifts or talents are just yet, don't worry. These exercises in this book will definitely help you figure them out. Learning who you truly are is a journey, and once you embrace the journey it can be quite fun.

About Larayne Glidewell:

Larayne Glidewell has been working with kids and newborns since she was the age of 11. Her passion carried over to her current positions specializing in children with autism. She is a therapist and teacher with the Next Step Academy as well as the Lead Coach for Junior Habitude Warrior Programs.

www.JuniorHabitudeWarrior.com

Assignment: Affirmations

In this assignment, write down at least 5 of your own affirmations:

1. _____

2. _____

3. _____

4. _____

5. _____

4

BUILD CONFIDENCE BY ENCOURAGING OTHERS

By Joshua Evans

Isn't it great to feel excited about something? Do you know that wonderful feeling you get when you find a new hobby or interest that you can throw all of your energy into? It's amazing to feel inspired by some new pursuit. In these times, even small words of encouragement can mean the world to us. It can be these small nudges that set us on a positive trajectory towards amazing success. Positive attitudes and encouragement are very useful in helping us and others build confidence. To truly live up to our potential, we must be confident in who we are and what we are doing. In life, many of us have wonderful influences that affect our attitudes and our successes. The best of these are the ones that are positive and encouraging. We must set a goal and work hard to surround ourselves with positive people who do good in the world. We also must aspire to be a positive influence on others. Who we choose to spend our time with is vitally important.

While we must work hard to surround ourselves with people that are supportive, it is even more important that we are supportive towards others through our words of encouragement and positive actions. Each of us carries the ability to build others up or to break others down. We must make the decision every day to be positive and helpful to others. We have the power to make people feel great about themselves or to become a bully. Every day we must make the choice to be a positive influence in other's lives.

Be careful. Sometimes, we are going to encounter people who are negative or pessimistic. It can be very difficult to maintain our confidence when someone else is working to make us feel less important or inadequate. Don't let them get to you! It is at these moments that we must stay confident in ourselves. If we are going to be leaders and role models for others, we have to overcome negative influences and keep our heads held up high.

One of the best ways to be more confident in ourselves is by helping other people. When we perform selfless acts of kindness, it can be a huge confidence booster! Many times we don't know the problems that others are facing, and we need to understand that our words can have a meaningful impact. So, the words better be positive! We must make the choice to help others. When we encourage other people it has a wonderful impact on them. It becomes a lesson for those that witness it. And, it will be a positive experience for you as well. Be confident in your efforts to help others and stay excited about the great impact that you are going to have in this world! Be honest and authentic with yourself so you can help others become their best selves as well.

3 Questions to Ask Yourself Each Day:

1. What is something you can do today to help someone else?

2. Who will you encounter today needing your encouragement?

3. How can you make someone smile today?

About Joshua Evans:

Joshua Evans works with high potential leadership teams and organizations to craft engagement-focused strategies for success. He is the CEO of Enthusiastic You! LLC, a bestselling author in Leadership/Management Training, a TEDx curator/host, an organizational engagement specialist, international speaker, and one of the leading experts on Enthusiasm. He is also a regular guest speaker and emcee at Habitude Warrior Conferences.

www.EnthusiasticYou.com

5

YOU ARE THE BEST!

By Jason Freeman

Do you ever lose sight of how brilliant and unique you are? I sure did. But, let me tell you a story. When I was a little kid, my folks told me that I was the best. As a youngster, so full of life, who was I to disagree with their words. However, in fourth grade, I changed schools and started noticing certain things about myself that drove me crazy. I observed that in gym class I tended to catch balls with my forehead, stomach, or glasses, instead of my hands. Wow, that was painful! I also became embarrassed that when I spoke, I always sounded like I had just come from the dentist where I'd been numbed up as if they were drilling for a cavity. I decided that I didn't like being different and that being different was bad. I let myself become miserable because I didn't like who I was. Now, when I am asked to speak at schools, students sometimes ask me if I was ever bullied when I was growing up. I start to shake my head no, but then remember that there was one big bully who pestered me day in and day out and wouldn't let up. Who do you think that bully was? That bully was me! While my parents were being good to me, my teachers were being kind to me, and my friends were being nice to me, I was busy being mean to myself and telling myself that I wasn't good enough.

When I was feeling bad about myself, I thought it would never end. I thought that I would always hate myself. But I was wrong! Today, I speak internationally to many groups and share the message that each one of us are great in our own special way!

The same speech impediment that I spent so much of my life hating, now inspires me and people around the world.

Our greatest challenges can indeed become our greatest gifts. You see, my parents were right! *I am the best!* It is your job to let your uniqueness and brilliance shine as much as you can. I know, unfortunately, this is all far easier to say than do. Here's a way I've found to begin letting your uniqueness and brilliance shine even when you feel frustrated with yourself. Pay attention to your breathing. Right now, put your hands on your belly. Feel it rise as you breathe in and get smaller as you breathe out. Concentrate on the sound of your breath and the feeling of your hands moving up and down. Do this for at least five minutes. If you are anything like me, the first time you do this simple exercise (it's actually a form of meditation), it will probably feel like absolutely nothing is happening. It may even feel like this meditation exercise is a complete waste of time. But, in reality, what you are doing has so many benefits. First, when you are concentrating on your breath, you are diverting your mind from thinking painful thoughts about yourself. Second, you are calming your mind so it has more freedom to notice your goodness and the goodness in the world.

Taking time to breathe in this way when you feel bad about yourself is a small step. But, small steps added together will take you where you want to go in a positive way! Remember, *YOU ARE THE BEST!*

About Jason Freeman:

At birth, Jason Freeman created a bit of a ruckus and lost oxygen in the process. As he grew older, he developed a one-of-a-kind accent, commonly called a speech impediment. Today, Jason is a bravery coach and an international speaker, traveling the world to inspire and motivate kids and adults to do their imperfect best. www.JasonWFreeman.com

CONFIDENCE! WANT SOME?

By Jenya Carter

Confidence! Want some? It's a daunting word, right? Confidence is a word that carries with it so much power; so many expectations. We always hear how important it is to have confidence in ourselves, to have confidence in our dreams, and to have confidence in our abilities. It sounds so simple to do.

All you have to do is simply close your eyes, and, magic, you are confident. Easy right? But, it's not always that simple. However, I've come to learn a little secret. You wanna hear it? Okay, here goes... believe it or not, deciding to be confident really *is* that simple! You just have to decide to do it. That's the first step. I know, it sounds crazy. I mean, I just gave a long monologue about the challenges of becoming confident and then I jump out and tell you that it's actually very simple to accomplish. Here's the thing. Having confidence in yourself and in your dreams is really something we can do right now.

It all comes down to a decision; your decision! Just like everything else we do in life, being confident comes down to making a decision to act that way. Lucky for us, we all make decisions each and every day from the time we wake up in the morning to the moment we go to sleep. This means that becoming confident will be a piece of cake to accomplish.

Walk through this with me... So our goal is to be confident, right? To have unshakable confidence? Here's how we're going to do it. Being confident comes down to 3 steps. Are you ready for them?

Step #1:

Make the decision to be confident! Decide that you are *AWESOME!* Decide that your dreams are awesome and that you are going to stand up very proudly!

Step #2:

Decide that you are enough and that regardless of any challenges, regardless of what others say or what you hear, that *YES, you can do it!* Decide that although you may fall down sometimes; although it might not always be easy, you must decide that you are capable, and you, your dreams, and your goals are worth it. This decision, in and of itself, is another form of confidence.

Step #3:

Realize that being confident is not always the easiest thing in the world, but that it isn't impossible either.

The 3rd and final step is for you to *decide to take action, no matter what!* Stick to your guns and remain confident, even when you don't feel like it and even when you have a bad day. Stick with it, no matter what. It gets easier each and every day.

Here's another secret for you. Just like having courage, overcoming challenges and being confident is a powerful thing. No, it is not always the easiest thing in the world to do. But, yes, you will have moments, as we all do, where you may feel down about yourself, your situation, or your dreams. This is simply a part of life, and each and every one of us has these moments… except me… (Just kidding, I'm human too!) However, you, dear reader, can do it. Being confident is not a huge task. It isn't some overwhelming superpower, and it doesn't take years of training to achieve. Being confident in yourself and in your life all comes down to deciding to do so. You will have moments where you slip up. That is normal. Being confident does not mean being perfect. Having confidence does not mean having all of the answers, or having the perfect results every time. Being confident comes down to appreciating and loving what you have. It means being proud of yourself, and your accomplishments. And, if nothing else, having confidence simply means being able to fake it until you make it, and taking some action to help you make it! Borrowing belief in yourself and your dreams from someone else for a little while is a good thing... until you build up enough belief of your own. If you are willing to go after something with everything you've got; if you are willing to set goals and take steps toward your dreams; if you are able to look in the mirror and tell yourself *"YOU ARE AWESOME,"*... then, you are confident! Because let me tell you, all of that, all of those beliefs, those efforts, it isn't easy. For you to be willing to be yourself and to keep moving forward even when things get tough, takes confidence. You, my dear friend, have it! You have confidence! Congratulations. Remember, it all comes down to making those decisions. Now, go conquer the world!

About Jenya Carter:

Jenya Carter is one of those amazing souls who's passion is to help kids see their true value and true potential! She connects with and mentors her young adults and kids to get their true results! Jenya is also one of our Junior Habitude Warrior Experts assisting us with our Junior Habitude Warrior Conferences throughout the world. Did we mention she is only 15 years old!

www.JuniorHabitudeWarrior.com

CONFIDENCE IS KEY IN EACH STAGE OF LIFE!

By Melisa Hall

Confidence is key to your life! There's a saying that goes like this: "I may not be perfect, but parts of me are pretty AWESOME!" Confidence is defined in the dictionary as the feeling or belief that one can have faith in or rely on someone or something. I believe that we are all fearfully and wonderfully made in the image and likeness of God and to truly be confident you must have faith and belief in Him and yourself to be pretty AWESOME! Your awesomeness comes alive when you become aware that there is something uniquely different about you. This unique difference is often revealed through something you can easily do or really love doing. It's a gift, talent, skill, or quality that only you possess and can do best. Sometimes, other people like your friends and family see it in you before you actually do; and sometimes you inwardly know that you have a superpower, but may not be sure how to express it. I also believe that as we grow from childhood to adulthood, there are certain traits of confidence that we all share and experience. However, this may not be fully expressed until we uncover or discover our own greatness. Confidence has a lot to do with how you feel within and not so much about what other people may think of you. It's about being happy with who you are and accepting the fact that you may not be able to do everything well, but there are some things you *can do* very well. It's about facing your fears and defeating your doubts.

As I prepared to write this chapter, I sat with my 15-year-old son Nathan and my 7-year old daughter Justice to discuss what they thought *confidence* is. Nathan said that he felt confidence is believing in yourself, not being afraid and doing what you had to do and not worrying about what others thought. Justice then proceeded to tell us of some things she wanted to do in her gymnastics class but was afraid to do them. Nathan and I began sharing our stories of when we were afraid and how we built the confidence and the faith and just did it anyway! Nathan had to sing a solo in front of his school for an assembly and was really afraid. He thought that his singing was not so good. He said after a while, with the support of good friends and family, he did it. But, again, he stated it was not so much about them, but it was more about how *he* felt.

The truth of the matter is, in my mind, he was correct. We can feel good that others feel great about us, but if we don't feel great about ourselves and what we can do then somehow it shows up in our actions. Allow me to share, very briefly, my story so that you can learn how to become confident and awesome.

As a little girl, I loved public speaking, debating and reading aloud in church and school. As I grew older throughout the years, I practiced and practiced and learned more and more about speaking. I am still learning even to this day. Thanks to people like Erik "Mr. Awesome" Swanson, I am now living one of my dreams by speaking in public internationally! At first, I was really scared to do it because there were so many other great speakers on the same stage who are very famous and popular and I wondered if I would ever be accepted internationally by them as well as the audience members. Many times in my mind, I would think that I had nothing too amazing to say. But one day I realized that it did not matter what others were saying, but rather it was what I was saying that people needed to hear. I started to believe that my voice and message could make a big difference in someone's life. For years, I always imagined in my mind that I would travel from the Bahamas to speak in front of large crowds and that they would love me.

But, what's more important is that I faced my fears and defeated my doubts. (Oh, and yes, they loved me!) Today, I am learning, loving and sometimes even laughing about how pretty awesome I have become with the help of God. I always remind myself about my favorite Bible verse to keep me confident each day: "I can do all things through Him that strengthens me." I have come to realize and accept the fact that I am not good at everything. Time ago I thought I needed to be that way. I am not that good at geography and directions, and maybe I will be better at it one day, but I refuse to let that stop me from feeling confident and pretty awesome about the other things I am really great at, especially when I grace the stage to speak! So, my question to you is … what are you great at? What are you afraid of? What will you do in the face of fear or doubt? Will you believe in yourself and have faith to know there are no limitations, no boundaries, and no restrictions as to where you can go or who you can become!? I want you to know that you have the power to be pretty awesome!

About Melisa Hall:

Dr. Melisa Hall is an certified international coach, speaker, teacher, and mentor. She is also a corporate & real estate attorney and an enterprising women's mentor and leader. Melisa is the author of the book "Declare Your Dreams". www.MelisaHallOnline.com

LEADERSHIP

Our definition of a true leader is one who shows others the way to success by inspiring and motivating them. A leader is the person who decides to step up and help others step up as well. A leader sets the direction for others and maps out where to go. A leader takes responsibility and always looks to do the right thing.

There are many different areas of leadership in life. You can start out by being a great leader among your friends and family. Then, you can lead in your community by doing kind things for people around your neighborhood. You can lead at school by assisting other classmates in learning and growing. You can offer to assist your teachers. You can volunteer to help out during upcoming school functions. You can become 'class president' in your school. You can volunteer to assist others by being a mentor to them and assisting them with their homework. There are many ways you can become a leader. On the next page, your assignment is to list seven ways you can become a leader.

Assignment:

LEADERSHIP

In this assignment, we would like you to write down 7 different ways you can think of that you can become a leader in your neighborhood and also at your school:

1. _____

2. _____

3. _____

4. _____

5. _____

6. _____

7. _____

LEADERSHIP! ARE YOU A GOOD LEADER?

By Sharon Lechter

Leadership!
Are you a good leader?

Good leaders use their influence to maximize the

efforts of others to achieve a common goal. You may have heard the phrase "he or she is a natural-born leader." While it is true that some people seem to display leadership ability at very early ages, I also believe that you can develop your ability to lead. Follow these 10 steps, and you can build your ability to influence others in a positive way.

1. Set a good example for others.

> When your friends or others around you see you using good judgement and achieving success as a result of the choices you make, they will want to be around you even more. They will also learn how they can become good examples for others.

2. Become an active listener.

> Great leaders know how to be good listeners. It is only by truly listening to others that you can learn what they want in life, and as a result you can learn how to successfully motivate them to take action toward success.

3. Think before you act.

> This will reduce emotional responses that you

may regret later. For instance, re-read emails and social media posts and ask yourself, "Does this communication help me or the receiver move toward a goal?"… "Is it a positive message?" If the answer to either message is "yes"… send the message. If the answer is "no," do not send it.

4. Acknowledge and celebrate the success of your friends.

By celebrating the successes of others, you are demonstrating true friendship. They will be drawn to you because you made them feel better about themselves. Use this power wisely.

5. Support friends in need.

A true leader will also recognize when someone needs a pat on the back or a helping hand. This generosity of spirit is essential in a great leader.

6. Participate in teams…sports or academically.

One way to learn leadership is through participating in team activities. Whether it is a team sport or a team project in school, learning to work together and accomplish a common goal will sharpen your leadership ability.

7. Read…and then read some more.

The more you know, the more you can contribute in a group setting. The saying "readers are leaders" is true because reading allows you to build your knowledge so you can share it with others. Reading also allows you to consider alternative perspectives besides your own.

8. Persistence pays...never give up.

Have you ever seen anyone give up…just before they were going to be successful? It is so sad. A true leader knows that it often takes several tries to become successful and is determined to not give up until he or she reaches that success.

9. Find a mentor...not an enabler.

Most great leaders are also great followers and know when and how to seek advice or counsel from other leaders. Look for someone who will guide you in the

10. Approach each task with enthusiasm.

> It is through enthusiasm that you can motivate others. They will see your excitement and desire for their success, and it will become contagious. Through your enthusiasm...they will become more enthusiastic.

You are already a leader. By focusing on these 10 steps you can become a great leader who listens, inspires and empowers others to achieve success. To your success!

About Sharon Lechter:

Sharon Lechter is a financial literacy expert, an entrepreneur, author, philanthropist, international speaker, licensed CPA and Chartered Global Management Accountant. She is the founder and CEO of Pay Your Family First, a financial education organization dedicated to providing the tools and mentorship to support families, women, and entrepreneurs. Credited as the genius behind the Rich Dad brand, Sharon is currently partnered with the Napoleon Hill Foundation. As a driving force behind these two mega brands, Sharon has demonstrated her entrepreneurial vision and business expertise and is the author of the bestselling books Think and Grow Rich for Women, Outwitting the Devil, Three Feet From Gold, and Rich Dad Poor Dad.

www.SharonLechter.com

10

THE 7 STEPS TO BECOME A LEADER

By Steve Beckles-Ebusua

Would you like to help others to do the right things? Would you like to set the direction for others? Would you like to be popular with everyone around you? If you answered 'YES' to all of these questions, then, that means you would like to become a leader!

Here are 7 steps that will help you become a young, awesome leader:

1. **Be confident!** But, be careful to not confuse confidence with arrogance. To do this, you need to fully understand what you are talking about. When you do speak, speak with conviction. However, if you are found to be wrong, admit it. When you do this, people are more likely to respect you and then follow you. **"The most beautiful thing you can wear is confidence."**

2. **Inspire** others to take action by leading by example! Commit yourself to being the best 'you' that you can be. Never let someone tell you that you cannot do something. If something isn't out there, go create it. There is no one like you. Just look at your fingerprint; out of 7.2 billion people on this planet, no one has your same fingerprint... **you are truly unique! "Inspiration is all about tapping into your inner thoughts and bringing them alive."**

3. **Be ambitious** and do not be afraid to take risks.

If you don't take risks, you can't grow. If you can't grow, you can't be your best. If you can't be your best, you can't be happy. If you can't be happy, what else is there? If you happen to fail, don't worry. It's just an opportunity to recognize your limitations and be better to adapt in the future. Only by knowing your limitations can you fully maximize your potential....so go for it! **"Be ambitious, as no one knows enough to be a pessimist."**

4. **Be organized.** In order to lead well, you must live well. Learn to be organized. If you are disorganized, you will be seen as unreliable, and people won't want to follow you.

5. **Be able to articulate** your thoughts and speech thoroughly and efficiently (a.k.a. communication skills). This also includes being able to delegate tasks and being clear about your expectations. **"When you open your mouth, you tell the world who you are."**

6. **Establish your goals** and commit to a plan of success. Structure, deadlines, and plans aren't

always the best way to lead. However, setting goals will always give you an indication of where you are and where you are not. It's difficult to get to a place you have not planned to get to. **"If you don't set goals, you will be working for someone else who does."**

7. **Take action now!** The best thing to do is the

right thing. The next best thing to do is the wrong thing. The worst thing to do is *nothing*. Don't let perfection become procrastination. Get things going by *doing*. **"Nothing happens until something moves."**

About Steve Beckles-Ebusua:

Steve is a dynamic, professional leadership speaker and Amazon Top 10 Bestselling Author. A great resource for schools, universities, and companies throughout Europe and USA.

www.TheSpeakerWithTheOrangeTie.com

11

SUCCESS SECRETS FOR EVERY YOUNG PERSON

By Scott Sorrell

If you want to skyrocket your achievement level in life, here are my "Success Secrets" that most kids (and even most adults) are clueless about. Do these and I promise that you will launch to amazing heights! Here are steps that will help you become an awesome leader:

1. Talk with adults! Do this often. Listen and participate in their conversations with each other. I see a big, positive difference in communication skills and life success between kids who mostly hang around and talk with other kids, and those who make it a habit of talking to lots of adults. And guess what, adults want to talk to you, too!

2. Become exceptional at something! Work hard to master at least one skill. Find something that will require a lot of practice and dedication, like a musical instrument, sport, or perhaps coding or drawing. When you've dedicated yourself to excellence in one thing and strive to be the best at it, you'll have an edge in life over people who have never worked hard to become amazing at something!

3. Read everything you can find! Read nature books, science fiction, biographies, business books, travel guides. Read e-books and online articles on politics, technology, and art. You'll experience 3 huge results: First, people will love talking with

you because you're knowledgeable. Second, you'll become a more articulate communicator, because reading increases your vocabulary. And third, your personal confidence will explode because of the first two!

4. Attend seminars, workshops, and conferences! I'm talking about serious learning opportunities, not just comic conferences. Go to personal development seminars and professional conferences. Your life will be transformed as you learn from experts, expand your personal vision, and get connected with other motivated people!

5. Speak in front of groups! This may mean getting *way* outside your comfort zone, but find, or even *create* opportunities to do public speaking. Start with a small group of friends or your class in school – or hey, run for office or class president! Then, work your way up. But, give speeches. Make presentations. Deliver talks. Pretty soon, you'll be seen as the expert everybody wants to know!

6. Smile! Do you think I'm goofy for putting this in a list of serious success habits? Trust me, this one practice will change your life. It will make people like you more, make them want to be around you,

and make them want to approach you with amazing opportunities. So, whether straight or not, or even with braces, let's see those teeth!

7. Start a business! It doesn't matter what kind of business you start, just start selling something. Come up with a service or product to offer. Magical things will happen later if you learn early how to persuade people to buy things, whether online or in person. So get selling!

8. Be a giver! Nothing is uglier than a self-focused person. Find charitable organizations or ministries to raise money for. Support worthy causes with your volunteer efforts and your own funds. And don't just give from your own surplus.

9. Write down your great ideas! Write them as soon as you have them. Personally, I like to dictate them onto an electronic device so that I don't lose them. For instance, I suddenly had a great idea and dictated this entire list in just 20 minutes while driving in my car. And I'm dictating this Number 9 in the parking lot after my arrival. Never lose your good ideas. Always use your time wisely!

If you make a habit of doing these nine simple, yet powerful steps, you will take your life from *ordinary* to *extraordinary*! Let me know when you do!

About Scott Sorrell:

Scott Sorrell is best known as "Mr. Charge Higher Prices," as he teaches his clients how to do just that and have their prospects thank them for it. Scott is also a professor at the University level, teaching kids in Entrepreneurship , Leadership, and Business Development.

www.SalesAdrenaline.com

12

LEAD YOURSELF & LEAD BY EXAMPLE!

By Dalí Melo

When I was a young girl living in Colombia at the age of 14 years old, I literally had nothing going on for me. As I entered high school, transferring from a Catholic girls-only school into a boys and girls public school, I was terrified, to say the least.

I was two years younger than everyone. I looked like the character Olive Oyl in the cartoon Popeye. I was dorky with a mixture of tomboyish charm and girly hints here and there. All in all, I was not ready to face this big transition in my life. In any school, there are always groups. I wanted to belong! I wanted to fit in any way I could. But, in my mind, I had nothing to offer. The fear of all the things that were wrong with me took a front seat in my mind. The very first day of school, I showed up with my sweater inside-out and let's just say the shoulder pads made a big fashion statement!

Obviously, this was not a great start. I went home and I played with my friends and then I decided to make a list of all the fantastic talents I had. This was such a great idea because it reassured me that: 1) my friends in the neighborhood really loved me! … And 2) I needed to reinvent myself.

The next day, confident and courageous as I was, I approached the cool kid's group. I had this whole thing planned in my head. I knew what I was going to say and how to act... but, all of the sudden, I panicked, and I heard myself making a long joke about my own sweater. Somehow, I ended up being myself again... *not* the cool girl I had planned the whole night before to be. But, wait! Surprisingly, one of the boys who was there, said, "My God, you are hilarious!" I answered, "Of course, I am!" That one sentence just came out of me because I honestly knew and believed that I truly was funny. I could make anyone laugh. That was one of my amazing talents that I had discovered about myself. So, that was my *in* with the cool kids! Being myself actually made me a very popular person in school. But, I didn't stop there. I also became a leader. I became a person people could trust and come to me for advice. Being courageous to be myself made me try out for many things. I started to write poetry. I was part of the debate team, dancing, and even singing.

I was unstoppable! These were my dreams and

priorities at the age of 14 years-old. I wanted to be liked! I wanted to be *someone*.

The story I just shared with you is as relevant now in my life as it was back then. I learned from very, early on, that I do not have to be someone *else* to belong. I can offer the best version of me; the person I have been working on so hard to become. I understand now that it takes a certain type of person to truly appreciate who I really I am. When we are at our most vulnerable and honest place is when big connections can happen. Today, as an adult, I look back at that fearful, little girl on that first day of high school, and I see a girl who learned that even as small as she was, she could still be loud enough to be heard and respected by others. Now, as a mother, I have to make important decisions and make important plans. I have to live by example. I want to have the moral compass to teach my son and to share with him all of my dorky stories. I want to show him that having confidence and being a leader in every stage of our lives takes practice. But, it's worth it! It does not matter if you are five inches or even a foot shorter than anyone. It doesn't matter if you have a funny laugh or have 'chronic clumsiness.' It only takes a moment to make a decision to be the best version of ourselves and to be whomever we want to be. After that, the universe helps take over!

About Dali Melo:

Dali Melo has been assisting kids of all ages for years, helping them find their true talents, gifts, and passions. She is also one of our Junior Habitude Warrior Leaders teaching kids from ages 8 to 18 in their Confidence, Leadership, and Personal Development. www.JuniorHabitudeWarrior.com

Assignment:

Your Talents & Gifts

In this assignment, write down 5 awesome talents and gifts you know you have that people love about you!

1. _____

2. _____

3. _____

4. _____

5. _____

13

PERSONAL DEVELOPMENT

What is *personal development?* Personal development is when you develop, work, and invest in yourself to be better each and every day. The more you work on yourself, the better you will become as a person and a great human being. There are many ways to develop yourself and build your character. Keep in mind, we are not saying that you need to become an expert at everything you set out to do. No, that's not what we are saying. What we are saying is that you can choose different areas of your life to improve on that will have an outstanding outcome for your future.

You should make a goal to become better, little by little, every day in a different area of your life. Here are some examples of some areas you can become better in, Studying at school; Homework; Reading; Learning new success strategies; Being a better listener; Being a kinder brother or sister; Eating more healthily; Working out and exercising.

Assignment:

PERSONAL DEVELOPMENT

In this assignment, we would like you to write down 7 different areas of your life you would like to improve and develop:

1. _____

2. _____

3. _____

4. _____

5. _____

6. _____

7. _____

JUNIOR HABITUDE WARRIORS

14

SMILE! YOU HAVE THAT CHOICE

By Ryan Lowe

I had the chance to fulfill a lifetime wish … to hear Tony Bennett sing the song "Smile." I have loved that song for years and had always wanted to see him perform in person. I had four or five opportunities, but something always came up. Finally, I was able to see him perform in New Orleans at the Mahalia Jackson Theater. After all these years, I couldn't believe I was going to hear my favorite singer perform my favorite song! My girlfriend and I took our seats in the balcony. I could hardly keep still. It seemed surreal.

This song has gotten me through more rough days and bad times than anything else. It reminds me to just *smile*, in spite of whatever happens. You know who originally wrote the song? It was the master of all comedians, Charlie Chaplin.

Smile though your heart is aching. Smile even though it's breaking.
When there are clouds in the sky, you'll get by. If you smile through your pain and sorrow, Smile and maybe tomorrow, You'll see the sun come shining through for you. Light up your face with gladness.
Hide every trace of sadness.
Although a tear may be ever so near, That's the time you must keep on trying. Smile, what's the use of crying? You'll find that life is still worthwhile...

If you just smile!

The song talks about tears and trying to remember life is still worth living. How could such a melancholy song be written by a comedian? The truth is Charlie's life was anything but a comedy. But, he kept smiling and decided to look at the bright side of life.

SMILE! Smiling doesn't mean you pretend everything's going right. Smiling is a choice to find the positive in every adverse situation and to deal with it in a mature way.

Here is the acronym I created for '**SMILE**':

Stop and think. Measure the problem. Identify solutions. Live and learn. Enjoy the outcome.

Smiling is a choice, and it's a lot easier to make that

choice if you're surrounded by things that make you smile. As you're surrounding yourself with positive influences, surround yourself with things that make you laugh. Hang around fun people, watch funny movies, and read books that put a smile on your face. It's easy to get sucked into other people's drama of watching negative shows and finding all the ways to be unhappy. But it's more productive to be around things that make you happy, not to mention a lot more fun.

About Ryan Lowe:

Ryan C. Lowe, The Positivity Pro, is a professional motivational keynote speaker, trainer & the author of the book entitled "Get off Your Attitude."
www.GetOffYourAttitude.com

15

CREATE HAPPINESS THROUGH SELF-LOVE

By Stacey Ellen

How do you create happiness, fulfillment, and success as your age? One of the biggest practices is through '*Self-Love.*' What does this mean, you may ask? Self-

Love is the belief that you hold that you are a valuable and worthy person. Our world is an outward reflection of what's happening within us, so that means the more you practice loving yourself and becoming your own best friend, the more you will see and experience love around you.

First, practice loving yourself no matter what happens in your life. Sometimes, things happen outside of our control. When I was about to graduate college, I was in a near-death car accident.

For years I lived with a very uneven face and smile and had to learn to love myself even though I didn't like what I looked like on the outside. The things that happen in your life don't define you, unless you allow it to. There is no one else like you here on this earth. You get to choose every day who you want to be and what you want to create. Leave the past in the past as it does not dictate what your future will be.

"What others say and think about you is none of your business." I heard that quote first from my mom as a child and it's so powerful. It doesn't matter if others like you or not. It's your job to like yourself. In turn, you will feel more confident and powerful as you build this muscle. I was bullied as a child and have been bullied as an adult as well. I don't take it personally though because people that feel the need to be mean to others are really hurting inside. They have their own wounds to heal so instead, I forgive them and send them love.

There is no one else like you here on earth. You have your own unique fingerprint, and your uniqueness is a gift. Take the time to acknowledge and understand these gifts that you have and your celebrate your inherent strengths.

Discover the things that bring you joy and that come easily to you. This can be done through journaling, working with experts, and taking steps everyday outside of your own comfort zone to experience something new.

Life is about practice, not perfection. As you take small steps to your big goals, know that failure is a part of learning and teaches us to redirect our efforts and move in another direction.

All of these things will build your confidence and

create an unstoppable foundation so you can achieve anything you set your mind to.

About Stacey Ellen:

Stacey Ellen is a certified Success Coach, Author, Speaker, and CEO of Stacey Ellen Enterprises. With a love for business, Stacey has worked with some of the country's top experts and helps people around the world learn their own personal RECIPE™ for success.

www.StaceyEllen.com

16

BUILD UP YOUR SELF DEVELOPMENT

By Justin Renner

Many of us are told at a young age to go to school, work hard in our classes and then graduate. Then, we are told to go to college, work hard in our classes, then graduate, get a job, and work hard for someone else. With all of this push from our culture and society to work, is there any encouragement for working on ourselves? Not really. In school it is all about competition. Competing with our classmates on homework and test grades. Feeling good or bad about ourselves based on our report cards. But, what if we could release ourselves from the pressure of having to conform to "the way things are?" Where is the way out of this cycle? How can I be unique in a world full of clones? The answer is

personal development!

I will never forget when my Dad made a decision that has changed the course of my life forever. Instead of getting upset at me about a low grade on my report card like he used to do, he stopped basing my potential on my test scores. Instead, he saw something greater in me.

He saw that I had a gift. I didn't think I had anything special, but I soon found out that I did. See, I have always been motivated by rewards, and he knew that. So, he challenged me to start reading personal development books and listening to motivational speeches by some of the greats (Les Brown, Jim Rohn, etc.) He paid me $2 dollars per video and $50 dollars for each book I would read completely. I hated reading. Being a hyperactive kid, reading used to be always so boring to me because my body wasn't going anywhere. But, I did love getting rewarded with extra spending money to help pay my bills (eating Taco Bell and buying new shoes).

But, after only a couple of months, I noticed an amazing improvement in my thinking. I wasn't thinking like my friends were. It was like I was on a higher level. I felt more confident about myself, and I knew deep down that I had a purpose for being on this earth. I knew that I had something special within me and it was my responsibility to manifest it.

Friends, coworkers, and family members started coming to me for advice and counsel for issues in their lives, and I was able to really help provide insight and clarity for them. Why? Because I was equipped. When others were goofing off and doing typical "teenage stuff," I was diving into books, CD's and teachings that accelerated my growth.

And the more I grew, the more I had to give, and that

is what this life is all about. Later, I went on to speak on big stages across the U.S and even in Canada providing humorous messages woven with inspiration. Speaking to rooms packed with 200 to 300 business men and women while I was still in high school was scary. But, I still felt equipped because I had grown to the level of being able to handle that. Had my Dad not started motivating me to enter into the vast world of personal development, I don't believe I would have been able to do what I did at the age that I did it.

I am 21 years old now, and I am an author of my best-selling book "The Book with a Hook" and a known inspirational speaker. I am also engaged to be married to the most amazing woman I have ever met. This is some big stuff and many people wonder how I am able to handle so much at such a young age.

I have to owe it to God for placing the greatness inside of me and for my mentors who have helped me discover it. So, my encouragement to you is to begin with reading just one personal development book, like this one, and start filling your mind with thoughts that you have never considered. My Dad used to pay me to read books. Now I can't stop paying to read them.

Personal development may sound *selfish*, but the truth is, it isn't selfish at all. The desire to be successful is not a wrong desire any more than a flower's natural inclination is to blossom. Through the process of personal development, you will discover that you have gifts and talents that you didn't even know existed. You have a purpose for being here that is bigger than you. You have a calling to make a difference in the lives around you and beyond. But, before you can change the world, you must start with changing yourself.

About Justin Renner:

Justin Renner is a 21-year-old author, international speaker, and presidential impersonator. He is currently pursuing a Finance degree at Texas State University and hopes to one day brighten the lives of millions of people. He is one of our Junior Habitude Warrior Experts.

www.JustinRenner.com

YOU OWN WHAT YOU KNOW

By Eric Lassard

Since a very young age, seven exactly, I had challenged all status-quo. All of them! The biggest challenge, however, was to challenge the age status. People may not judge you by your race or believes, or at least not all of the time. But, they will definitively judge you by your age.

The questions are always inevitable: How old are you? What grade are you in? So, you immediately get classified. They will put you in a box. In the box, they keep the image and memories of themselves at your age. Immediately this triggers them to remind them how they felt at that age. Ultimately, they will look at you with either love and empathy, or they will just ignore you. It took me many years to figure out. I soon learned a lesson… to not only be non-judgmental but, I learned to not judge people by any means or anatomical or physiological parameters.

I also figured out that if I met people on the phone first, or Facebook messaging, and just have a chat with them, then two things usually happen when they found out my age. Either they get inspired or they get intimidated. If they get inspired and accept that even at my age you can know more than expected, immediately we create a mutual friendship and partnership. If they get intimidated, they typically run away. My mother always taught me not to run after trains or people. She says that there is always another one coming.

You may ask the question: "Why is it so important to

be accepted?" I asked many people this question and they always tell me that it one of the most important things in life. In business, if they do not accept you, you have no chance to get through. They marginalize you and leave you there. They do not trust you. They do not respect you. You become an outcast. No one wants to become an outcast! If you know me, you'll know I love to be challenged! Personally, I love the challenges of questioning ideas and beliefs that are so strongly embedded in people's mind that people do not even bother to analyze them. They just believe that it is right because other people believe that it is correct.

Over the years, I did understand that beliefs are like dreams. You know that dreams are great, but unless they do not become goals they will always just stay dreams. The same goes with beliefs. If they do not become absolute knowledge, then they will simply stay merely iffy beliefs. The only way to make your beliefs into absolute knowledge is to experience them for yourself. Once you experience them, then they become your absolute, defined knowledge. This knowledge is all yours. Your experience. It is unique.

It is only yours, and nobody can take it from you. You can lose everything you have, like money, your home, credibility, loved ones, but nobody can take from you what you already know. Get into the habit of questioning everything and challenging all your beliefs until they become *knowledge*. *You own what you know!*

About Eric Lassard:

Eric Lassard started his business career at the young age of 7 years old. Now, he is a bestselling author, motivational speaker, startup founder, owns multiple businesses, is a social entrepreneur and the founder of Air School. Did we mention he is still only 12 years old?!!!

www.EricLassard.com

BUILD A BULLY-PROOF LIFE

By Chris Warner

I Am Bully-Proof

Today, I take a stand! Today, I forbid you to treat me secondhand! Today, I make my own demands! No more back downs! No more shakedowns! No more sad-faced clown! I stand strong and proud, and THIS ENDS NOW! Let's get along or let's not, either way. . . Today, THIS WILL STOP! Because from this day forward, I AM a Junior Habitude Warrior and I AM Bully-Proof!

Live Bully-Proof is a mantra – a battle cry if you will and my gift to you. It will serve to strengthen your resolve, establish your confidence, build your self-esteem, and fortify your courage. It will protect you as you tackle your daily challenges. Most importantly, it gives you the inner-strength to stand your ground and face your bully head-on.

Every morning, I want you to stand *powerfully* (feet planted, head high, shoulders back, chest out, fists clenched) in front of your mirror, look yourself square in the eye and repeat this battle cry aloud three times in a strong, commanding tone.

Your life is no game and your well-being is no joke. Live Bully-Proof is some of the most effective, thoroughly proven advice ever developed. It will make you feel better about yourself and the choices you make. It will put an end to bullying for good and it will improve the overall quality of your life beyond belief!

The most effective way to put an end to bullying forever is to permanently grow your self-confidence. We accomplish this by making you strong, both mentally and physically - it really is that simple.

Life doesn't get easier - you just get stronger. To succeed in life requires commitment, discipline, and dedication.

You are much stronger than you could ever imagine! Turn your pain into power. Harness negativity, channel it and use it to your advantage. If you practice and implement what Erik "Mr. Awesome" Swanson and I preach every single day, then you will conquer your fears, crush self-doubt, and have absolute control over your own life!

When you combine your *habits* with your *attitude*, you create what is referred to as 'Habitudes.' By engaging in a daily, habitual routine, you armor up and Bully-Proof yourself automatically. These daily habits positively affect your attitude and before you know it, you are a bonafide **Habitude Warrior**! Your confidence will grow and your attitude will become exponentially bolder. It will build hope and carve a path toward all the cool, new things life has in store for you!

You are very important to the world! Without you,

the universe would be unbalanced – incomplete. In the history of time, there will never be another *YOU*, so let's do our best to make sure that you and your life is 100% AWESOME!

Each day of your life, no matter what the challenge is, always remember this sage piece of advice - "If you want to be strong, learn how to fight alone." Armor up, believe in yourself, stand your ground and always *Live Bully-Proof*!

About Chris Warner:

Chris Warner is an American Actor, Professional Keynote Speaker, and a Youth Mentor. Chris works with children and schools to teach his Live Bully-Proof system.

www.LiveBullyProof.com

Assignment:

LIVE BULLY-PROOF

In this assignment, write down 3 statements you can say to someone who is trying to bully you in any way.

1. _____

2. _____

3. _____

19

GOALS ARE IMPERATIVE

By Logan Langemeier

Goals are something that every person needs to have, whether you are a famous athlete like Tom Brady or if you're an 8-year-old kid. The sad truth is that even after people set goals in their lives, they seem to give up on those goals that they just set, or never finish them. Someone might look at you and say that you are being too ambitious. Let me tell you right now, any goal you set and you have a passion for, and you put your mind to it, you can achieve it! There will, of course, be some failures and heartache. But, you must continue and pursue them! It will take time and effort, but you can achieve it, and it will be worth it. Trust me! Always remember that nothing worth having comes easily.

Now, there are many different types of goals that you can set. Short-term and long-term goals are just two of the major types. Both of these type of goals should always be 'SMART.' Short-term goals should all lead up to one of your ultimate, long-term goals. Long-term goals are the final big picture goal you want in a specific area of your life. To get you to the big, long-term goals, you should have many little step goals, which are your short-term goals. You will have great success by implementing the 'SMART' system of goal strategies. 'SMART' is an acronym that I follow when setting a goal.

S - Specific; always make it a specific goal. I want to play college football is not as specific. You need to include in your goal the team, the division, the position that you want to play. I want to play

Division-1 NCAA football at Baylor University as left tackle! That's a specific goal.

M -Measurable; You want to keep a measure and check to make sure that you are consistently getting closer to that specific goal.

A - Attainable; Do you have or know what needs to happen to attain the goal? You want to know the time and the resources to attain it.

R - Realistic; Is this goal something that you can reach or is this a goal that you cannot finish without some help from others. You need to be honest with yourself at this step and really ask what needs to happen to accomplish the goal and is it realistic? And finally,

T -Time; You will need to have a start date and an end, completion date for your goal. This will keep you on track. Another one of my long-term goals in my life is to become a pilot. Now, I will have many short-term goals (or steps) to achieve that long-term goal.

When you are setting up your goals, make sure to write them down and look at it every morning. This will keep you on track and thinking about it throughout the day. Always have it available to see to remind you. Make your goals 'SMART' and make them *AWESOME*. That's how you become a *Junior Habitude Warrior* and ultimately a *Habitude Warrior!* Never give up on your goals and don't take any days off. You deserve it.

About Logan Langemeier:

Logan is a true inspiration! He can easily be found teaching and mentoring the youth throughout the nation. Logan is one of our amazing experts at our Junior Habitude Warrior Conferences. Check out the Conference at:

www.JuniorHabitudeWarrior.com

20

YOU ARE THE BEST!

By Erik "Mr. Awesome" Swanson

Decide early in life to live by a *'Positive Mental Attitude'* You have that choice! It's completely up to you. Either way, things are going to happen each day. It's totally up to you to choose the way you think throughout each day. Stop allowing other people to rent space in your mind. Remind yourself each day and in front of every challenge: "How would a positive leader think and feel in the midst of this experience?"... Then act and emulate it. It sounds simple, doesn't it? Guess what, it really is that simple! Maintaining a positive attitude and truly believing that *I am the best* has really changed my life for the better! People now call me by the nickname **"Mr. Awesome"** because I'm so positive all of the time. Being so positive literally rubs off on others and makes the world spin just a bit nicer each day. Be someone's *Awesomeness!*

The Power of Nicknames

What's your nickname? Do you have one? Get one! All Superheroes have one. Aren't you a Superhero? Ask your parents and your friends what they would call you if you had one. I've had many nicknames over the years that suited me during those times. One of my first was given to me by my friends in Texas. They used to call me **"*Styles*"** because I always seemed to have my own style of doing things which made me fun to be around, they said. Then it changed to *"Mr. Brightside"* as I always look at the bright side of things and rarely complain. Now, my nickname that was given to me by our good friend and motivational speaking legend, Les Brown, is now *"Mr. Awesome!"* Great nicknames make you very memorable… and that's what you want. Make sure you pick a positive nickname. You want to stand out in a crowd.

Become a Superhero!

The Power of the

60 Second Morning Mirror

Take 60 seconds every morning while you are brushing your teeth and look straight into the mirror. Stare straight into your eyes and say these words:

I am the best! I am the best! I am the best! I am the best!

I AM THE BEST!

You need to pump yourself up every morning to make it an awesome day. The more you say, **"I AM THE BEST"** to yourself every day, and throughout the day, it will start to seep into your sub-conscious mind and allow you to start believing that you truly are the best. Who else better to pump yourself up than yourself? Keep being *AWESOME*!

The Power of
Visualization

Visualization means to literally 'see' it first in your mind before actually seeing it in reality. But, the cool thing is that you can manifest anything in your mind in any direction you would like it to show up. So, it's your choice. Be bold. Be awesome. Be super positive with your visualization. Studies tell us that visualization truly works. Your sub-conscious mind cannot really tell the difference between what is real and what you are visualizing. Try it right now. Just close your eyes and take a few minutes to visualize something you would like to come true in the near future. Keep doing this each day and then take actions towards that goal.

BOOK ERIK

'MR AWESOME' SWANSON

To book Mr. Swanson to motivate and speak to your company, association, school, or church group feel free to contact us at

www.SpeakerErik.com

or email us at

team@HabitudeWarrior.com

SWANSON'S CREED !

I am the best
I am focused
I will succeed
I believe in myself
I have the will to win
I set high expectations
I visualize my perfect future
I don't let others bring me down
I surround myself with winners
I will learn and grow everyday !

ABOUT ERIK

SWANSON

Erik Swanson has delivered over 6000 motivational presentations at conferences and meetings worldwide. As an award winning International Keynote Speaker, Best-Selling Author & Attitude Coach, Erik Swanson is in great demand! Speaking on average to more than one million people per year, he is both versatile in his approach and effective in a wide array of training topics.

Respectively nicknamed "*MR. AWESOME*" by many who know him well, Erik invites some of the most talented and most famous speakers of the world to join him on his coveted stages, such as Brian Tracy,

Nasa's Performance Coach Dr. Denis Waitley, Motivational Legend Les Brown... From the book & movie 'The Secret,' Bob Proctor, Jack Canfield, John Assaraf, & The Millionaire Maker Loral Langemeier, Co-Author of 'Rich Dad Poor Dad' Sharon Lechter. Mr. Swanson has created and developed the super popular *Habitude Warrior Conference* which boasts a 2-year waiting list and includes over 33 top leaders around the world in a 'Ted Talk' style event, which has quickly climbed to one of the top 10 events not to miss in the United States!